SUEÑO

A Play in Three Acts
by
JOSÉ RIVERA

An adaptation of
DON PEDRO CALDERÓN DE LA BARCA's
Life Is a Dream

Dramatic Publishing
Woodstock, Illinois • London, England • Melbourne, Australia

*** NOTICE ***

The amateur and stock acting rights to this work are controlled exclusively by THE DRAMATIC PUBLISHING COMPANY without whose permission in writing no performance of it may be given. Royalty fees are given in our current catalog and are subject to change without notice. Royalty must be paid every time a play is performed whether or not it is presented for profit and whether or not admission is charged. A play is performed any time it is acted before an audience. All inquiries concerning amateur and stock rights should be addressed to:

DRAMATIC PUBLISHING
P. O. Box 129, Woodstock, Illinois 60098

COPYRIGHT LAW GIVES THE AUTHOR OR THE AUTHOR'S AGENT *THE EXCLUSIVE RIGHT TO MAKE COPIES.* This law provides authors with a fair return for their creative efforts. Authors earn their living from the royalties they receive from book sales and from the performance of their work. Conscientious observance of copyright law is not only ethical, it encourages authors to continue their creative work. This work is fully protected by copyright. No alterations, deletions or substitutions may be made in the work without the prior written consent of the publisher. No part of this work may be reproduced or transmitted in any form or by any means, electronic or mechanical, including photocopy, recording, videotape, film, or any information storage and retrieval system, without permission in writing from the publisher. It may not be performed either by professionals or amateurs without payment of royalty. All rights, including but not limited to the professional, motion picture, radio, television, videotape, foreign language, tabloid, recitation, lecturing, publication, and reading are reserved.

For performance of any songs and recordings mentioned in this play which are in copyright, the permission of the copyright owners must be obtained or other songs and recordings in the public domain substituted.

©MCMXCIX by
JOSÉ RIVERA

Printed in the United States of America
All Rights Reserved
(SUEÑO)

ISBN 0-87129-935-6

IMPORTANT BILLING AND CREDIT REQUIREMENTS

All producers of the play *must* give credit to the author(s) of the play in all programs distributed in connection with performances of the play and in all instances in which the title of the play appears for purposes of advertising, publicizing or otherwise exploiting the play and/or a production. The name of the author(s) *must* also appear on a separate line, on which no other name appears, immediately following the title, and *must* appear in size of type not less than fifty percent the size of the title type. *On all programs the following should appear:*

*"Produced by special arrangement with
THE DRAMATIC PUBLISHING COMPANY of Woodstock, Illinois"*

All producers of the play must also include the following acknowledgment on the title page of all programs distributed in connection with performances of the play and on all advertising and promotional materials:

*"SUEÑO was originally commissioned and produced by
Hartford Stage Company, Hartford, Conn."*

"Beauty will be convulsive — or will cease to be."

— André Breton

"He realized that, though he may penetrate all the riddles of the higher and lower orders, the task of shaping the senseless and dizzying stuff of dreams is the hardest that a man can attempt—much harder than weaving a rope of sand or of coining the faceless wind."

— Jorge Luis Borges, *The Circular Ruins*

"La vida no es sueño."

— Federico García Lorca, *The Poet in New York*

A Dance with Calderón

This is the story of a relationship.

I knew very little about *Life Is a Dream* when I got a call from the Hartford Stage Company asking if I had any interest in adapting the play for "next season." In fact, I hadn't even read the play by the time I called the theatre a few weeks later to say I'd do it.

A month later, when I stopped procrastinating and finally *did* read *Life Is a Dream*, I understood why this great play—written by one of the most gifted and prolific dramatists in history—is so rarely performed in North America.

Something in its stubborn density, its enigmatic elegance, its obsessions, the odd codes of human behavior embedded in its verse...something about this story of a resurrected prince who questions the nature of existence...something in this marvelous, sprawling, insanely technical play seemed more distant, more difficult, more untranslatable than anything I knew from Aeschylus. Remote and modern, dark and wacky, poetic and pungent, stuffy and sexy, *Life Is a Dream* terrified me. I wanted to call Hartford Stage and suggest another playwright for the job.

But at the same time that the play spooked me, it attracted me. There's greatness in this awesome tale. There's beauty in Segismundo's fiercesome search for the meaning of life. There's dignity in Rosaura's cross-dressing, cross-European pursuit of justice. There's something sobering and moving in Basilio's attempt to come to a redemptive peace between the dictates of the stars and his love for his son. This is a play full of Big Questions. What is honor? What separates man from the animals? If life is a dream, what happens to free will? If life is a dream, who's dreaming it? I knew I couldn't pass the job on to another writer. I did the next best thing. I procrastinated for another six months. "Next season" at Hartford Stage came and went.

When I actually *did* start to write, I was faced with an undeniable fact: I had never adapted a play before and I didn't know where to start. I asked myself: What do I have to contribute to *Life Is a Dream*? The obvious answer was: Nothing. I was stuck (again) until I shifted the question slightly: What do I have to contribute to a modern North American audience's appreciation of *Life Is a Dream*? That was the shift in perspective that finally got me going.

Practical questions asserted themselves right away. Do I change the play's time and location? Do I set it in Pinochet's Chile? Franco's Spain? Castro's Cuba? Clinton's America? I rejected these ideas as too gimmicky. The original play is set in Poland—a choice akin to Shakespeare setting his play about two gentlemen in Verona. I opted to set the play in Spain in 1635, the time and place of its creation. As a Latino writer aware of the relationship between ancient Spain and the New World, it was exciting to me to imagine this play springing from a society simultaneously obsessed with honor at home and genocide and conquest of indigenous people abroad. When I began to imagine the characters of this play in relation to the New World, I felt I had a "way into" the play that a contemporary audience might appreciate.

I then turned my attention to the play's bizarre plot. That was easy. I imagined that most theatregoers had a *right* to know and enjoy Calderón's narrative. So I decided to be faithful to the original story, almost moment by moment, with only a couple of structural changes, and some (potentially radical) re-examining of the ending of the play.

The bulk of my work centered around an article I read which said that Calderón wasn't interested in writing *characters* as we understand that word today. Calderón (according to the article) wrote archetypes, walking mouthpieces without full-blown psychologies. So I tried to recreate Calderón's play with 20th-century characterizations. I asked myself fundamental questions about Segismundo's internal reality. Did he ever hallucinate while in isolation? Was he ever baptized? Has he ever felt love? Did Basilio ever visit him? How did the King keep his son's identity a secret for twenty-five years? Has the Prince ever seen his own face?

Calderón never answers these questions. In attempting to invent an internal reality for *all* the characters, I reconstructed the language of the play. I cut the lengthy asides; I trimmed the long speeches. And I did away with most of Calderón's metaphors and created new imagery with a contemporary feel.

Segismundo's jail cell is now a "sewer pipe," he refers to himself as "a storm of chemical responses pretending to have a soul," and as "the soul of anthrax and polio." Basilio calls the stars "secrets of the universe written in nightly Braille" and "the dandruff of Zeus." Estrella tells Rosaura that Astolfo's manliness "does something truly wacky to my personal chemistry." Rosaura refers to her horse—a "violent Hippogriff" in some translations—as an "instinct-challenged freak." She calls Spain "morbid and feisty all at the same time." Her servant Clarín asks, when they arrive in Spain: "What contaminated mirage, I wonder, will come along to pick our pockets and flog our imaginations?"

And the famous end-of-act-two speech now reflects a contemporary world's end-of-century skepticism—a point of view unthinkable in Calderón's very Catholic Spain. Segismundo says: "What is life? A frenzy. What is living? An illusion, a shadow, a fiction. The greatest good is nothing but a weightless idea. To live is to sleep, to live is to dream, all who live are dreamers, all dreamers are the dreams of God—and what is God Himself, but the greatest dream of all?"

As the months went by, I found my relationship to Calderón changing. Someone once told me that to write an adaptation is to serve an apprenticeship with a master. Like any good apprentice, I approached the Old Man with awe mixed with fear. This was followed by familiarity as I chipped away at the many translations of this play in pursuit of its beating heart. This was followed by a strange irritation at Calderón's repetitions, his limited vocabulary, his recycled metaphors, his slavish devotion to the conventions of his time, his unwieldy subplot, and his obstinate championing of the status quo. This was followed by a truly oedipal desire to kill the old bastard. But eventually, when it was all said and done, I returned to a newborn respect and came back full circle to true awe; that is, awe *without* the fear.

For ultimately the story of an adaptation is the story of a *relationship*. It's either a dance, a dialogue, a duet, or a duel between you the adaptor and the original creator—for Calderón and me, it's been all of the above.

— José Rivera

SUEÑO was produced by Hartford Stage Company in Hartford, Conn., on February 20, 1998. It was directed by Lisa Peterson and included the following artists:

Artistic Director	MICHAEL WILSON
Managing Director	STEPHEN J. ALBERT
Set Design	MICHAEL YEARGAN
Costume Design	MEG NEVILLE
Lighting Design	CHRISTOPHER AKERLIND
Original Music and Sound Design	DAVID BUDRIES
Fight Director	DAVID LEONG
Dramaturg	MORGAN JENNESS
Production Stage Manager	DEBORAH VANDERGRIFT
Casting by	BERNARD TELSEY CASTING
Flying by	FOY

THE CAST

Rosaura	MICHI BARALL
Clotaldo	YUSEF BULOS
Estrella	ALENE DAWSON
Clarín	JAN LESLIE HARDING
Segismundo	JOHN ORTIZ
Servant	KEN PARKER
Basilio	GENO SILVA
1st Soldier	SAM WELLINGTON
Astolfo	DAMIAN YOUNG
Soldier, Guards, Servants, Voices	DARIN DUNSTON, JOHN SOCAS

SUEÑO was commissioned by Hartford Stage Company, Mark Lamos, Artistic Director. The world premiere production was sponsored by Aetna, the Hartford Foundation for Public Giving, and the National Endowment for the Arts.

SUEÑO

A Play in Three Acts
For 7 Men and 2 Women, extras

CHARACTERS

BASILIO............................. King of Spain
CLOTALDO .... his advisor, Rosaura's father
SERVANT
ROSAURA .... a young woman
CLARIN .... her manservant
SEGISMUNDO.......... Prince of Spain, son of Basilio
ASTOLFO......................... Duke of Warsaw
ESTRELLA............................. a princess
1ST SOLDIER

and...
SERVANTS, SOLDIERS, TOWER GUARDS, AND PRISON VOICES

TIME: 1635.

PLACE: Spain.

Running time: 2 hours, 15 minutes.

ACT ONE

SCENE ONE

SETTING: *King Basilio's castle. Midday. The sun and the moon are about to achieve a total eclipse.*

AT RISE: *BASILIO and his advisor CLOTALDO are in their 40s. BASILIO looks over the sheets of parchment he's holding in his hands.*

BASILIO *(re the parchment).* His horoscope tells us he'll be born a monster.

CLOTALDO. And if the stars are wrong, Your Majesty—?

BASILIO. Wrong? The sun itself weeps blood! It fights for its life against a ferocious moon. See for yourself: it's the worst eclipse since the Crucifixion! Buildings shake. Rocks fall from the clouds. Trees spontaneously burn. Night lasts forty-eight hours. Strange new constellations pollute the night sky with unreadable portents. Have you ever seen anything like it?

CLOTALDO. Only in my dreams.

BASILIO. Every astrologer in the kingdom predicts my son will grow up to be a cruel, tyrannical, and outrageous prince. He'll cut the kingdom in two in an endless and tragic civil war. And he'll trample my dishonored corpse on his way to the throne!

CLOTALDO. But stars can only point the way to the future, sire, they can't create it. They can bend the will but they can't force—.

(A SERVANT enters carrying a BABY wrapped in a bloody blanket.)

SERVANT. King Basilio. Your son.
BASILIO. The queen?
SERVANT. Dead.
BASILIO. Dead!
SERVANT. The boy burst through her body, cutting her off from the living world.
BASILIO. She's killed by her son! He's baptized in her blood! This creature is already a man, Clotaldo. He's repaid goodness with cruelty. His first living act was murder. What do you say now?
CLOTALDO *(taking the BABY)*. He has your eyes, sire.
BASILIO. God of Love, how do I solve this? How do I rewrite this creature's destiny? How do I save Spain—and myself? *(BASILIO exits. The BABY cries.)*
CLOTALDO *(to SERVANT)*. Is there any milk in the castle? *(A total eclipse plunges the stage into darkness.)*

SCENE TWO

SETTING: *Twenty-five years later. A mountain. A tower. The tower door is opened.*

AT RISE: *ROSAURA, 25, robust, clever, loud, dressed as a man, tumbles onto the stage, landing hard on her back. At her side is an ornate sword.*

ROSAURA *(on her back, in pain).* Violent, mixed-up horse! Unnaturally stupid mammal! Instinct-challenged freak! *(She picks herself up and yells at the offstage horse.)* I swear if you were a bird you wouldn't know how to fly! If you were a stream you wouldn't know how to babble! You're a fart without smell! A religion without God! A dreamer without sleep!

(CLARÍN, her manservant, enters, his fingers in his ears.)

CLARÍN. I see your lungs are still working, madam.
ROSAURA. Did you see that dumb beast throw me? Ran to the edge of the cliff—and something scared it—like it hit an invisible wall and couldn't go on! It stopped and the momentum knocked me down the mountain so hard, it practically left me blind.
CLARÍN *(looking).* Good, otherwise you'd have to watch *both* our horses taking off!
ROSAURA *(seeing it).* Get back here! No, *dammit!* It's as if they *know* something about this dismal place.
CLARÍN. Maybe they're not as stupid as we look, huh?
ROSAURA. Shut up. Maps?

CLARÍN. In the saddlebags galloping back to Poland at, oh, fifty miles an hour.

ROSAURA *(looking around)*. Brilliant! Lost! Lost in some ugly desert...some freak frontier...look at it, Clarín. Illogical stone formations, creepy craters—the place looks like the backside of the moon.

CLARÍN. Food, drink, and shelter would be nice, huh?

ROSAURA. You're a dreamer. Is it Spain? It looks vaguely Spanish: morbid and feisty all at the same time. Hey, Spain! Is this how you stamp the passport of every new immigrant to your country—in blood? *(No answer.)* But since when have the lost and dishonored of the world ever found pity?

CLARÍN. Horseless, stranded, wronged, overburdened, screwed, molested, tampered with, addicted to stress, fucked in the head...

ROSAURA. Sun's going down. Add "cold" to your list of miseries.

CLARÍN. Darkness! Ask yourself: what queer tricksters and fiends accompany the darkness of Castile? What contaminated mirage, I wonder, will come along to pick our pockets and flog our imaginations? I miss Poland! It's over, madam! We're doomed! Oh fuck it, let's have a little sex before we die! *(CLARÍN goes to embrace ROSAURA. She easily pushes him away as she sees the tower.)*

ROSAURA. Either I've started dreaming or I've succumbed to hypnosis or I've been hit by the arrow of some aimless sorcerer...but in the sun's last shy rays, I see... I don't know *what* I see...

CLARÍN. I don't know either, but I see it too.

ROSAURA. A palace? Too decrepit. A fortress? Too solitary. A home? Too unhappy.

CLARÍN. Prison. I know the smell.

ROSAURA. Yes, a prison carved into the stubborn architecture of the mountain—camouflaged by walls of rock—so no one'll ever notice it. A labyrinth so well-hidden the sun's perfect eyesight has no way of seeing it. Recommendation?

CLARÍN. A closer look. Let's give the owners a chance to wine and dine a pair of starving hobos.

ROSAURA. How do I look?

CLARÍN. Manly, madam—sir!

ROSAURA *(approaching the tower)*. That door...looks more like a wound than a door. Or it's the deep uterus out of which midnight's darkness itself is born. Or the cave from which nightmares enter the world of the sleeping... *(The sound of chains.)*

CLARÍN. Chains of a prisoner? A slave? Or a ghost?

SEGISMUNDO *(off)*. Ay misero de mi! Y ay infelice!

CLARÍN. It's a baby's cry!

ROSAURA. A poor unborn man crying from his cradle of stone.

CLARÍN. Rosaura, I'd like to leave this hoodoo place! I know this pitiful cry means nothing but tricks and suffering and really, really bad, bad torments. *(A weak light appears at the door. ROSAURA looks in.)*

ROSAURA. A brief, doubtful light...shows me a dark habitat...and—Clarín!—the ghost of a poor man—no, more *reflection* than ghost: a walking mirage, born dead, dressed in animal skins...a slave, maybe, stolen from an oppressed island, or a refugee of a defeated warrior-state where nightmares are rulers and imaginary monsters walk the streets.

CLARÍN. Poor thing. His only companion is the exhausted light and the dead silence of the mountains.

ROSAURA. And us.

(SEGISMUNDO, 25, a wild man dressed in animal skins, arms and legs bound with chains, holding a lantern, appears in the tower.)

SEGISMUNDO. God of Love, God of Light, are you listening? If you exist, tell me: what law have I broken today? What have I done to deserve this punishment? I'm told that birth itself is a sin. I was born once, I think. Therefore I understand I'm being punished for my original sin. And since you're a just God—so your books tell me—then I know I deserve the full heat of your punishment. But aren't all men born with original sin? Aren't all men guilty? And if all are guilty of the strange crime of being born, shouldn't all men be enslaved as I am? Yet, I know from my small experience of the world that some men are actually free. Free! Yet here I am! Why? What have I done to deserve this? Birds are free. Birds are beautiful. Is it their beauty that exempts them? I've never seen my face. Am I unfree because I am unbeautiful? But wild snakes are ugly! Yet they are free! It isn't mere ugliness, then, that imprisons me, it's something else. My ugliness goes deep. It's an ugliness of the soul. And it must be contagious. I must have something that will infect the body of the world, that's why I must be quarantined like this, like a secret medical experiment, God's wild new virus kept under strict control. I am the soul of polio and anthrax! Yet even now...in this degenerate state...why should I, a man made vaguely in God's image...why should I, who have more soul and better instincts and greater will and more life than a bird or a wild snake or a simple germ...why should I be less free?

ROSAURA *(sotto to CLARÍN)*. Those unhappy words break my heart.

SEGISMUNDO. Who's out there? Who's listening to me? Clotaldo?

CLARÍN *(sotto to ROSAURA)*. Say yes, and don't tell him about me! *(ROSAURA steps forward. CLARÍN remains hidden.)*

ROSAURA. A poor traveler, forlorn and dishonored like yourself... *(SEGISMUNDO hurls himself at ROSAURA. She goes for her sword. He disarms her. He holds her. He covers her eyes with one hand and squeezes. ROSAURA screams.)*

SEGISMUNDO. I'll tear your eyes from your head for having seen too much of the world and too much of me!

CLARÍN *(hidden)*. I'm a blind old ghost and I haven't seen a thing!

ROSAURA *(struggling)*. If you were indeed born a man and not a monster, I know all I have to do is kneel before you and you'll give me mercy. *(SEGISMUNDO lets go of ROSAURA's face. But he holds her arm. He explores her body with his hands. He sniffs her.)*

SEGISMUNDO. Your voice...is that what they call "melody"? Your face...is that what they mean by "art"? Are women and oceans this beautiful? These are your eyes. There's light in them...is that what the stars look like when seen by a free man? Your confusing skin...this is human skin...not the cold iron of the inquisitor. Blow!

(SEGISMUNDO holds his hand in front of ROSAURA's mouth and she blows.) Is that like the wind? Is that a hurricane? Is that the rain? Say your name.

ROSAURA. I can't.

SEGISMUNDO *(laughs).* It doesn't matter. Your curses would sound to me like the opening notes of Creation. In the Beginning were the words: "I can't." *(SEGISMUNDO presses his thumbs into her throat.)*

ROSAURA. Sir! No! *(He stops.)*

SEGISMUNDO. This box is my crib and my grave. This sewer pipe is all I've ever known. I've been a bag of guts, a storm of chemical responses pretending to have a soul, eating and shitting and waiting to die! All this time I've spoken to one person. A dark man whose face I've never seen. Clotaldo gives me advice—he tells me how to hold my dick so I don't piss on myself! He tries to describe women to me! And courtship. And violin playing. And government. And honor. He tells me of the wonders of an Eden discovered beyond the Ocean Sea. I dream some day I'll be exiled to that New World, to live among my kind, the noble savages at one with nature, on pure land ten times the size of Europe! Clotaldo hears all my thoughts. He's my silent diary, taking in all my dreams, my confessions and worries. He teaches me to read the Bible! He tells me, there, between the lines, there is the flickering light, the shining residue of God's glory. God's actual *fingerprints* are there in the space between Psalms, between the screaming heartbeats of the suffering Christ on the cross. Yes! And I've learned my language by listening to those delicious words: "glory," "grace," "resurrection," "redemption,"—gentle words that soothed my wrists and ankles, when I was a boy, like pure water poured on bloody wounds. Yes! But the years have passed so slowly. And that black book has taught me a world I would never see beyond this black box. One day I grabbed the book from Clotaldo and I tore its pages and put them in my mouth and I ate them. I ate them! Chapter and verse! I chewed those holy, phony sentiments, swallowed them whole, and shit them out again. I've been eating Bibles and shitting Gospels all my life. The words are written in my tissues now. In the blood vessels of my brain. In the hollow rooms of my mind, lining the walls with lies and promises! *(SEGISMUNDO grabs his head as if experiencing searing pain. Subsiding, he looks at ROSAURA.)* Sir, your voice has quieted those cunning words. Your skin is the only texture these depleted fingers have ever enjoyed. My thirsty eyes know it's poison to drink you in but they can't help themselves. They are dying to see that which will kill them to see. But I don't care! Let me look at you—more natural than all the Nature I've seen fornicating from my narrow window—you, the gift of life—and let me die!

ROSAURA. My eyes and ears amaze me today: they show me and tell me about wonders I've never heard or seen before. I don't know what to say, or what to ask first. All I know is this: today Heaven dropped me here and brought me comfort, if it's possible to be comforted by someone more desperate than yourself. My mother told me a story of an ancient scholar who was so poor he lived on the few blades of grass he could collect from the field. And one day he said, "could any man be poorer and sadder than me?" He turned around and saw his answer. There he saw an older man, his mentor in fact, picking up the scraps he had thrown away. I've been living in misery, cursing, asking God, "Is there anyone else who suffers as much as I do?" Now you've given me the answer. I know that my pain would be joy to you and you'd receive it gladly. So if I can give you any comfort, sir, let me do it by telling you my own desperate story.

SEGISMUNDO. I sensed it! Someone has wronged you, sir. Someone has dishonored you.

ROSAURA. Yes, but the first thing to know about me is this: I am not a...

CLOTALDO *(off)*. Guards! Careless, foolish guards!

CLARÍN *(hidden)*. Great! More confusion!

ROSAURA. What's that?

SEGISMUNDO. That's Clotaldo, my mentor and tormentor!

CLOTALDO *(off)*. All intruders are to be arrested at once!

CLARÍN *(hidden)*. My God, we're fucked!

(CLOTALDO, 1st and 2nd TOWER GUARDS enter. CLOTALDO wears a mask. The GUARDS carry masks and firearms.)

CLOTALDO *(to the GUARDS)*. Hide your faces! *(The GUARDS put on their masks.)*

CLARÍN *(hidden)*. Costume party with guns!

CLOTALDO *(to ROSAURA)*. What have you done? This place is prohibited to all by order of the king! *(To the GUARDS.)* Arrest him!

SEGISMUNDO. Don't hurt him, Clotaldo! I swear to God I'd rather tear out my own eyes than watch my friend suffer.

CLOTALDO *(to SEGISMUNDO)*. Arrogant Segismundo, your miseries are so great that by God's orders you died before you were ever born. You died in the paralyzed womb of your nonmother! You're a ghost, Segismundo, a flicker of reflected candlelight, and you must remain silent and invisible. *(To GUARDS.)* Take him inside! *(The GUARDS grab SEGISMUNDO. He resists. They disarm him and beat him.)*

ROSAURA *(retrieving her sword)*. Don't hurt him!

SEGISMUNDO. Throw me in your deepest pit and I will rise up against you!

(The GUARDS drag SEGISMUNDO offstage. CLARÍN is found by the 3rd GUARD and pushed onstage.)

ROSAURA *(to CLOTALDO)*. Seeing how much arrogance offends you, sir, I'd be wrong not to humbly beg for my life. Please be moved by pity for me and my companion...

CLARÍN *(to ROSAURA)*. If neither humility nor pride moves him, well, it's been nice knowing you.

CLOTALDO *(to 3rd GUARD)*. Take their weapons and cover their eyes.

ROSAURA *(before anyone can touch her sword)*. This sword once belonged to a nobleman. I yield it to no one, sir, but you. No one below your rank may touch it.

CLARÍN. My sword, on the other hand, can be manhandled by any Spanish son of a bitch you can find. *(To 3rd GUARD.)* You, for instance. *(CLARÍN offers his sword to the 3rd GUARD who, insulted, slaps CLARÍN across the face. ROSAURA jumps the 3rd GUARD and is re-

strained by CLOTALDO. The 3rd GUARD drags the stunned CLARÍN away.)

ROSAURA. He's a poor old man! What kind of dishonorable nation insults and injures a harmless old clown?

CLOTALDO. Your sword, sir.

ROSAURA *(swallowing her rage).* If we're going to die... let us die with honor. I give you my sword as a testament to your mercy. It's a weapon of uncountable worth and must be respected, even if my life is not. *(ROSAURA hands CLOTALDO the ornate sword. He stares at it in disbelief.)*

CLOTALDO. What is happening to me...?

ROSAURA. That sword has a great secret and a great power; it's drawn me to Spain to avenge a wrong done to me...

CLOTALDO. Who gave this to you?

ROSAURA. A woman I knew.

CLOTALDO. What's her name?

ROSAURA. That's a secret.

CLOTALDO. More secrets! And how do you know this sword has secrets too? And powers?

ROSAURA. The woman who gave me this sword said to me: go to Spain and find some way, through your natural genius, to make this sword known to the nobility there. I know, once this sword is seen, that one of the noblemen will favor you, and claim you as his heir.

CLOTALDO *(turning pale).* ...Which man?

ROSAURA. Full of superstitions and afraid he had died, she wouldn't repeat his name. *(CLOTALDO walks away, examining the sword in his trembling hands.)*

CLOTALDO *(to ROSAURA).* I'm bound by my oath of loyalty to the king who said, twenty-five years ago, that anyone caught trespassing on this unlucky mountain must be put to death. Even if...my own dear son...were to break this law...and die as a consequence of my actions, my duty is to my king, a duty that beats louder than my heart.

ROSAURA. Sir, you look at me with such sorrow...

CLOTALDO. It's as if my heart, sensing the presence of a kindred spirit, has run up to my eyes to see you, forcing my tears.

(The 1st and 2nd GUARDS enter.)

ROSAURA *(not understanding)*. Sir?

CLOTALDO. I don't know which of us has the greater trouble, my friend. *(To the GUARDS.)* Bind him. *(The GUARDS hold ROSAURA. Blackout.)*

SCENE THREE

SETTING: *Basilio's palace.*

AT RISE: *DUKE ASTOLFO and PRINCESS ESTRELLA enter from opposite sides of the stage.*

ASTOLFO. Goddess of Starlight! Aurora borealis! Solar flare! Daughter of Apollo! Of Rainbows! My soul, my happiness, my love, my war, my light! I could go on. Your voice is a flute! Your heart, a timpani! Your blood vessels are little pipes. Your corpuscles, little notes...to disembowel you would be to write a symphony in blood! One more time. A metaphor will do. Flowers are dishrags compared to you! Antelopes? Clumsy inedible venison compared to you. Helen? A slutbox. Aphrodite? Maggot poop. In short, you, Princess, are stronger than the musk-oxen, wiser than the Joshua tree, more industrious than the ants of the Amazon. Let me try that again. You are more poignant than the cross on which our savior suffered and died, more pointed than the thorns which pricked the divine brain, more forceful than the nails uniting God and humanity in a Crucifix of Understanding, and more delicious than the ultimate reunion He enjoyed with His Father...

ESTRELLA. Thanks, thanks, I think I get it.

ASTOLFO. But I haven't gotten a chance to praise each of your breasts—individually.

ESTRELLA. Cool off, Duke. It's bullshit. Your words are flattering but they contradict your actions. Everywhere I look I see the machinery of war and the naked exercise of power politics. Pure destruction is your aim, Astolfo, not love; it's conquest, not peace, that you want. *(She starts to leave.)*

ASTOLFO. Hear me out, *señorita*! Eugtorgius III was King of Castile. Basilio was his son. Basilio had two sisters: one was your mother, dear cousin, one was mine. Both grand dames are dead. Okay. Here it gets baroque. Basilio is old and feeble. He's inexplicably remote. Spends his nights watching cloak-and-dagger mysteries or gazing at indecipherable modern paintings. His mind is nearly shot through with illusions and hobgoblins that could easily ruin the kingdom. His wife died twenty-five years ago in childbirth. That child is dead. Being more in love with astrology than sex, Basilio never remarried. His only heirs, unfortunately, are you and I. Your claim rests on the fact that your mother was the older of the two sisters and that you actually live in Spain. My claim, alas the superior claim...

ESTRELLA. ...rests on the accidental fact that you were born with a penis.

ASTOLFO. Perhaps in some future, distant century—the postmodern 18th or 19th centuries—a penis will not matter. But this is today, my dear, and we have to be realistic.

ESTRELLA. Get to the point.

ASTOLFO. Our declining uncle-king said he'd judge which of us is the proper heir to the Spanish throne. That's why I've left my native home in Poland to come here today. But it's not to make war, as you think, it's to offer a compromise.

ESTRELLA. I'm waiting for it.

ASTOLFO. Do you believe in love at first sight? Do you believe the gods of love are greater than the gods of war? Each of your breasts is a New World, Estrella, a world more fecund, more laden with gold and glory than the endless New Worlds discovered by your sailors. Let me finish. My compromise is this: let's preempt our doddering uncle by getting married. Let's surrender totally to the gods of love. I'll be crowned king. You'll be my proud queen. We'll seal our claim to the throne in the damp, sticky bed of state, and rule Castile and the New World as one heart, one soul, one body.

ESTRELLA. Language has a strong effect on me. Your language is quite potent. I want the crown, Astolfo...and since I can't grow a penis to get the crown, perhaps I'll use yours instead. So if wanting you will get me some power...I might be talked into it...yes, I can feel myself beginning to want you... *(They get closer and closer. They nearly embrace, then she pulls back.)* ...though I have to say your eloquence on behalf of love is contradicted by the sexy girl's picture you wear around your neck! Animal!

ASTOLFO. I can explain that...

(KING BASILIO, now mid-60s and weak, enters. Mentally he's in and out. ESTRELLA and ASTOLFO go to him.)

ESTRELLA. Wiser than Jesus!

ASTOLFO. Nicer than Socrates!

ESTRELLA. Nicer than Jesus!

ASTOLFO. Wiser than Socrates!

ESTRELLA. We kiss your feet!

ASTOLFO. We lick the ends of your toes! *(They attempt to, but BASILIO stops them.)*

BASILIO. I am moved by your sincerity, children. Come—niece, nephew, embrace the old body. Estrella, a little closer please. A little tighter. Just a bit more. You both love me! That's so nice. You should love me. I'm a great king and I have a great kingdom to give away!

ESTRELLA. Wiser than Jesus!

ASTOLFO. Nicer than Socrates!

BASILIO. But first I have something very important to tell you both. It weighs on me. Oppresses me greatly. Silence is all I ask of you at this moment of truth. You know I am called Basilio the Learned. I am called Basilio the Great. I am referred to in the epic poetry of Castile as Basilio the Beautiful. I like that last one very much. It's true, I run an empire in decline. A New

World was given to us by God and we've depopulated it completely, pulled the last golden turds from its exhausted asshole, and have nothing to show for it but syphilis, the Reformation, and the disdain of history. Still, we must go on! Anyway, you know I love mathematics. You know I'm a numerologist and can, by studying numbers in various relationships, tell the future. Basilio the Man Able to See the Future through Mathematics, I believe, is what they call me. You know I study the stars. You know the stars have many names: angels' tears, the perspiration of God, piercing rays of divine love, ancient pearls, light-infused originators of dreams, wish-fulfillers, tablets of mystery, dandruff of Zeus, secrets of the universe written in nightly Braille, the pressure points of Heaven, skyfire. They have been the object of my obsessive study and contemplation because they are the secret pages upon which God Himself types our future. A future very few—a gifted few—the geniuses of our time—are able to read. Children, I am such a man. Thank you, thank you. *(Beat.)* Twenty-five years ago my wife died giving birth to a freak. I told the kingdom that its prince had died. It's a lie. I built a secret tower in the mountains, on the outskirts of the kingdom, among distant cliffs and sterile boulders where sunlight never reaches. I published strict laws declaring nobody may enter the forbidden zone around those hills. In that tower, my unhappy son, this human viper, destroyer of my hopes and dreams, *lives to this day.*

CLOTALDO *(voice over)*. He has your eyes, sire.

BASILIO. Untrustworthy doctors and astrologers who witnessed the birth of Segismundo were killed on my orders. Clotaldo himself killed them. Further, Clotaldo's been the child's secret guardian, teaching this newborn tiger language, bringing him the word of God and the precepts of the one true Catholic church. Throughout my reign, there have been rumors of a secret prince. In fact my enemies have searched the countryside for him. Sightings of false Segismundos have occurred all over Castile. Rumors and rumblings keep me up at night and frighten me. *(Beat.)* I have three thoughts today. First, I love Spain, my Spain, very much. It was to spare Castile the rule of tyranny that I secluded my deformed child. Second, I have denied the prince his freedom and his rights. And that denial does not agree with Christ's teaching which says that in order to prevent tyranny I need not act like a tyrant myself. Third, it's possible I've made a serious mistake. What if all those prophecies, astrologers, all that number-crunching, those eclipses and omens were wrong? It's possible he's *inclined* to tyranny and harsh violence, but it's an inclination easily civilized by reason, kindness and prayer. For we all know the stars only point the way to the future—they don't create it. That task can only be fulfilled by One, by a God who's ordered that man's will be free, free to choose good over evil, free to think free thoughts. Here's my thinking. It will stun you. You think one of you will become supreme leader of Spain. Sorry—tomorrow I will place my son Segismundo on my throne instead. Without telling him he's my son, he'll be dragged out of prison and placed on one of the most powerful thrones the earth has ever known. He'll have absolute power to govern and command you. Three things may happen. First, he'll be kind and intelligent and will disprove the prophecies of the neurotic stars. If that's so, you'll enjoy his enlightened reign. Second, he'll be cruel, monstrous, and proud. He'll be the one-man holocaust the bloody eclipse predicted twenty-five years ago. If that happens, I'll reimprison him instantly. Third, if that happens, I will abdicate the throne and make way for you two, Astolfo and Estrella, radiant king and queen of the Spanish state.

ASTOLFO *(stunned)*. Is that what you really want?

BASILIO. It is my will. Do you question it?

ASTOLFO. If that's your will, let cousin Segismundo appear!

ESTRELLA. Let's meet this sudden and lucky new king!

BASILIO. Go to your rooms. It'll take a while to release my son from his chains, dress him, and make him ready. Tomorrow! Tomorrow you'll visit with the king!

ASTOLFO. Long live great King Basilio!

ESTRELLA. Long life—and sanity—to the king!

(ASTOLFO and ESTRELLA kiss the KING's hand and exit. CLOTALDO, ROSAURA and CLARÍN enter.)

CLOTALDO. A moment, dear sovereign?

BASILIO. A moment for you, old friend? A lifetime! Speak.

CLOTALDO *(on the verge of crying)*. Countless times I've come to you full of joy, and today, of all days, could've been my happiest.

BASILIO. Why is it we old men are always on the verge of crying?

CLOTALDO *(indicating ROSAURA)*. That handsome boy has entered the forbidden tower and he's seen Segismundo. I know that means certain death. But he showed me an ancient sword which I had given to my dear Violante before I left her and broke her heart—I have an overwhelming feeling this boy is my...

BASILIO *(laughs).* You're a lucky man, Clotaldo! If this crime had occurred twenty-four hours ago it would have meant the death of your friends. But today the sad secret of my unfortunate boy has been revealed. It doesn't matter who knows it now. See me later. There's much I must tell you. There's much you must do for me. You'll be my right-hand man in the most amazing act of government the world has ever seen. These friends you bring before me? Pardoned unconditionally.

CLOTALDO. May they praise your merciful name for a thousand years! *(BASILIO exits. CLOTALDO goes to ROSAURA and CLARÍN.)* Friends, you are free. *(ROSAURA kneels at CLOTALDO's feet.)*

ROSAURA. I kiss these feet a thousand times! I mean that sincerely. *(CLARÍN doesn't move.)* Clarín?

CLARÍN. I'm still deciding.

ROSAURA. Get down and start kissing! *(CLARÍN kisses CLOTALDO's feet.)* You've given me a new life, sir. Please give your lifelong slave his first command!

CLOTALDO. No, I haven't given you a life. Any young man of breeding, once he's been offended as you have, has stopped living. You have no life until you've regained your honor—which can be done—honor can be cleaned spotless—but it's something only you can do.

ROSAURA. What I must do to resurrect my fortunes is find swift, final, and if necessary, *deadly* revenge. Once my honor is cleaned in the blood of my enemy, my life will return to its former glory.

CLOTALDO. Take your sword. A sword that was once mine—I mean, mine while I had it in my hands today—

knows how to avenge a wrong. *(ROSAURA gratefully takes the sword.)* Your enemy, is he a great man?

ROSAURA. He's so great, in fact, I can't repeat his name.

CLOTALDO. But if you tell me his name you'll inspire me to fight with you.

ROSAURA. As I don't want you to think I undervalue your courageous offer to fight with me, I'll tell you. The man who wronged me—correction, *ruined* me—is no less than the great Astolfo, Duke of Warsaw.

CLOTALDO *(taken aback)*. Astolfo.

ROSAURA. May the faithless hog be butchered and roasted a thousand times a day! I mean that literally!

CLOTALDO. But, my young Lord, if you're Polish, then the good Duke of Warsaw is your lord, and a lord can never offend a fellow noblemen.

ROSAURA. Even though he is my peer, he has disgraced me.

CLOTALDO. But he wouldn't dare slap a nobleman's face.

ROSAURA. His offense to me, sir, was far greater than a slap to the face... if you understand me.

CLOTALDO. I do not.

ROSAURA. I'll tell you a secret. I don't know what force of gravity draws me to you. Or why I feel an instant melancholy, an organic sympathy, when I look in your eyes, a sadness strangely mitigated by profound respect. This force forces me to speak. Look in my eyes, sir. Run your hand along the soft curves of my face. Listen to the strange pitch of my voice. Though I possess the swords and daggers of a man... I lack his "ultimate weapon."

CLARÍN *(grabbing his own crotch)*. Get it?

CLOTALDO *(getting it)*. *Ay cielos!*

ROSAURA. Ask yourself: isn't it the ultimate insult for Astolfo to come to Spain to marry Estrella though he's had relations with me? He's dirtied me, sir. He's disqualified me from the clean, legitimate bed of every nobleman in Europe. I've said too much! *(On the verge of tears, ROSAURA exits. Lights out.)*

SCENE FOUR

SETTING: *Hours later. The tower.*

AT RISE: *SEGISMUNDO stares out a small window, crying. CLOTALDO, wearing his mask, enters with food, drink, and books.*

CLOTALDO. I won't leave until I see you eat and drink.
SEGISMUNDO *(wiping his eyes).* Is there anything greater than freedom, Clotaldo? If there is something—is it honor? If I had my honor would I be able to endure this?
CLOTALDO. I can't answer that.
SEGISMUNDO. What *is* honor? How do I know I have it?
CLOTALDO. Honor is...like that eagle you see flying out there...who disdains gravity and flies from the earth to the heavenly ether like a quick fire, like lightning escaping the hollow clouds, like an ascending rocket.
SEGISMUNDO. I understand it now. Honor is a metaphor.
CLOTALDO. Drink. *(CLOTALDO offers the drink. As SEGISMUNDO drinks, the drug effects him quickly. The lights begin to fade on him the sleepier he gets.)*
SEGISMUNDO. What is honor to a prisoner? There is greatness in me, Clotaldo! Armadas and armies in me! I

am a prisoner only by force. If I had my freedom, I'd bow to no man...I'd bow to no man...I'd bow to no man...

(SEGISMUNDO passes out. CLOTALDO looks at him as the masked GUARDS enter.)

CLOTALDO *(to SEGISMUNDO)*. It's going to be a dark night, my prince. And all I can see in this terrible darkness are clouds and eclipses and amnesia. It's like a calming, killing gas is blanketing the sky... *(The GUARDS unchain SEGISMUNDO and lift him on their shoulders. Blackout.)*

END OF ACT ONE

ACT TWO

SCENE ONE

SETTING: *The next day. The palace.*

AT RISE: *CLOTALDO and BASILIO enter.*

CLOTALDO. Segismundo's sleeping in your bed, sire, lethargic, oblivious; when he awakens, the machinery of state is poised to honor and serve him as if he were Your Majesty. Will you now tell me your purpose in this?

BASILIO. Can my experiment change Fate? Can it challenge the stars? Can I, a free man, made in God's image, alter my own son's destiny and prove that the astral prophecies of two decades ago were false? Today Segismundo will learn he is my son. He'll learn he's heir to the Spanish throne. He'll learn the extent of his absolute and riveting power. Then we'll see. He'll show us by his actions what he's been dreaming of doing all these years. If he's an enlightened despot he'll be allowed to remain. If he's a tyrant then he'll be sent back to his chains and his solitude.

CLOTALDO. Why did you command that I drug him? Why bring him to the palace asleep?

BASILIO. If he fails this test and must be forced back to that miserable life, knowing *he's* the real king, he'll surely lose his mind. But he fell asleep in his cell before coming here. And he'll reawaken in his cell if necessary.

Thus we'll be able to tell him he only dreamed he was king. And he'll accept that, knowing, as we all do, that all who live are dreamers.

CLOTALDO. I don't know if you'll succeed in this, sire, but it's too late now. He's been awakened and may be approaching.

BASILIO. I must withdraw. Speak to him, gentle friend, teach him, as you have all his life. Be the golden thread that guides my son through his personal labyrinth.

CLOTALDO. Do I have permission to tell him it was you who ordered him imprisoned at birth?

BASILIO. If he knows everything, he'll understand all the dangers involved in this experiment, and he'll succeed.

(BASILIO exits. CLARÍN enters.)

CLOTALDO. Where's your master—your mistress? What's she-he doing?

CLARÍN. She's a she again. And she's dressing the part. Rosaura's decided, since she's come out of the closet, that she'll now raid that closet for the finest girl's clothes in the kingdom.

CLOTALDO. That's proper and good.

CLARÍN. And she's changed her name. And she's lied to everyone who'll listen. She's told everyone she's your niece. And that little white lie has sent her stock through the roof. She's now an honored lady-in-waiting to the nubile, eye-pleasing, come-hither Estrella.

CLOTALDO. That's good. As her uncle I can legitimately be responsible for her honor. She'll derive her honor strictly from me.

CLARÍN. Yeah, that too. One more thing. About that other thing. The revenge thing. She says she agrees with you and she's going to bide her time and wait for the perfect moment for the two of you to gang up and kill you-know-who for doing you-know-what to you-know-who. Am I clear on this?

CLOTALDO. Yes. Simply waiting is the best thing she can do right now.

CLARÍN. Everybody in this damn court is so agreeable! As for *me*, well, the world seems to have forgotten me—faithful Clarín who's tagged behind that stark, ungovernable girl for less than minimum wage for too long! But I tell you, sir, if I don't get something to *eat*, and *soon*, I'm going to sing like a friggin' canary and expose the whole lot of you double-dealers and flakes to every hack poet who'll listen to me!

CLOTALDO. Be my slave and you will eat every day.

CLARÍN. Not perfect. The slave part is not perfect...

(Music plays. SEGISMUNDO enters, accompanied by the SERVANT carrying a full-length mirror. SEGISMUNDO, wearing the formal clothing of a prince, gazes at himself in wonder.)

SEGISMUNDO. *Ay Dios*, what am I seeing? *Ay Dios*, what do I feel? What's this dreadful beauty? Why do I doubt it and believe it? God of Love, is this your son Segismundo? Is this me wearing silk and golden studs—and *shoes*? Is this me surrounded by lucid and spirited servants? Is this me among so many people dying to dress me and address me as "Your Lordship"? They say dreams are wonders. Wonders enchant and deceive. But

I know I'm awake! I know, somehow, I am now splendid Segismundo! God, I didn't know what it was like to walk without chains! My God, please, if this is your promise of the future, keep it! Don't take it away from me! I've dreamed of this day all my life—and now—it's happened! *(CLOTALDO approaches SEGISMUNDO.)*

CLOTALDO. Give me your hand and let me kiss it, sir. I am honored to be the first among the nobles of Castile to pledge you unconditional loyalty.

SEGISMUNDO. Your voice. You're Clotaldo, aren't you? How is it possible? How can the man who mistreated me in prison be *here*, pledging his allegiance to me?

CLOTALDO. In the great confusion your new state creates in you, you experience a thousand natural doubts. But I wish to free you from that, if I may. You are, sir, the king's son, the prince, and the principle heir to the Spanish throne. You were secluded at birth and hidden in a desert tower because astrologers looking into your future predicted a thousand tragedies if you were ever to wear the crown. But trusting that your strength of character could vanquish the prophecies of the stars—because a magnificent soul can conquer anything—you've been brought to the king's palace from the tower in which you languished. This was done while you slept, while your soul was resting and peaceful. Your father will come to see you and from the king, Segismundo, you'll learn the rest.

SEGISMUNDO. Lawless traitor! Hypocrite! Subversive! What else do I need to know, now that I know who I really am? You, Clotaldo, you have betrayed your nation by concealing me!

CLOTALDO. *Ay de mi triste!*

SEGISMUNDO. You've degraded the royal family and rebelled against the law! You've been unnatural and cruel to me! Now, as king, as Law, and as myself, I condemn you to die by these very hands! *(The SERVANT gets between CLOTALDO and SEGISMUNDO.)*

SERVANT. Your Majesty!

SEGISMUNDO. No one will hinder me! I swear to God if anyone gets between us...

SERVANT *(to CLOTALDO)*. You must go!

CLOTALDO *(to SEGISMUNDO)*. I feel sorry for you, my son. You have the chance to prove yourself. But if you're barbaric and fierce, everything you see and feel will disappear. *(CLOTALDO exits.)*

SERVANT *(to SEGISMUNDO)*. Sir, I must say something...

SEGISMUNDO. I'm pleading with you to shut your mouth!

SERVANT. By keeping you in the tower Clotaldo was only obeying the Law of the king!

SEGISMUNDO. If the king's Law stinks it should not be obeyed!

SERVANT. Clotaldo didn't question the Law or his king.

SEGISMUNDO. I predict a really hard time for anyone—*anyone*—who contradicts me today.

CLARÍN *(to SERVANT)*. Listen to your prince, fool!

SEGISMUNDO *(to CLARÍN)*. And who the hell are you?

CLARÍN. Oh, just an old clown with a big mouth, a fly, really, a dust particle...

SEGISMUNDO. Well, you're the only thing in this dreamlike world that makes me one bit happy.

CLARÍN. Can you translate that sentiment into food?

(ASTOLFO enters.)

ASTOLFO. May you achieve a kind of orgasmic happiness a thousand times a day, oh Prince! Soul of Spain! Subduer of the Maya! Tamer of the Taino! Sovereign of the Old World, the New World, and the Next World! You have emerged from the hot belly of those mountains like Christ clawing his way up from hell: a human sunrise, a resurrected hope, a Spanish Orpheus.

SEGISMUNDO. May God help you.

ASTOLFO. Uh-huh. Obviously you don't know who I am. That's the only excuse you have for not honoring me with a little more passion and a lot more language. Here's a hint. I am Astolfo, Duke of Warsaw. Your cousin? We're equals?

SEGISMUNDO. If I say, "May God bless you," haven't I honored you enough? Watch yourself, or next time I'll greet you with, "God save me from this fucking idiot!"

(ESTRELLA enters. She has written her little speech on a piece of paper which she reads.)

ESTRELLA. Majestic Father of the Spanish Civilization. You are most welcome to this throne which gratefully receives the round warmth of your royal rump and breathlessly desires union with you. Despite all the prophecies, which ranked you somewhat lower than Caligula, we know you will be a potent, plentiful, and penetrating prince. Curtsey. *(ESTRELLA curtsies. SEGISMUNDO has never been this close to a woman. He gets closer to ESTRELLA.)*

SEGISMUNDO *(to ESTRELLA)*. Who are you, Princess? Who is this fallen angel—wingless, almost human—one part dirt, one part blood, one part starlight?

CLARÍN. *Cousin*, sire, the girl's your *cousin*...

ESTRELLA. Estrella is my name...

CLARÍN. ... ambition is my game.

SEGISMUNDO. Many good things have happened to me, Lady. Blinders have been taken off my eyes. Fetters have been removed from my legs. I've climbed the long road from hell to heaven in a day! But nothing has been quite as glorious as this glorious moment with you.

ESTRELLA *(getting closer to him)*. You have a way with words.

ASTOLFO *(to SERVANT)*. If he touches her hand, I'm lost! *(SEGISMUNDO roughly grabs ESTRELLA's hand and kisses it violently.)*

SERVANT *(to SEGISMUNDO)*. Sir, what you're doing violates every single convention...

SEGISMUNDO. Didn't I tell you to get out of my way?

SERVANT. But she's Astolfo's Lady. You insult him by—

SEGISMUNDO. I am the Law now. I am convention. There can't be any insult if I do what makes me happy!

SERVANT. But you said yourself if the Law stinks it shouldn't be obeyed.

SEGISMUNDO. Every word out of your mouth is treasonous! Can anyone tell me the punishment for treason?

SERVANT. You can't punish me! I've been in this house all my life! I watched you being born! I watched your mother die!

SEGISMUNDO. I can't? Did you say I *can't*? *(SEGISMUNDO grabs the SERVANT. He sticks his thumbs into the SERVANT's eyes until they bleed. Blinded, bleeding, the SERVANT staggers out of the room. ESTRELLA, shocked, follows him. ASTOLFO stares at SEGISMUNDO whose hands are bloody.)* I think I can.

ASTOLFO *(shaken).* Your Majesty...there's a difference between men and animals...that difference is Law...and Law is the codification of self-mastery and self-restraint...

SEGISMUNDO. Shut up, Astolfo. You're a blowhard and a bore. Relax, you don't want to lose your head over this little matter, do you?

(BASILIO enters.)

BASILIO. What's happened here?

SEGISMUNDO. Nothing's happened here. No one of any importance has been troubled here. Nothing interesting has been lost. *(Holding out his bloody hands.)* Here are his eyes.

CLARÍN *(to SEGISMUNDO).* Excuse me, but that's the, you know, king?

BASILIO *(horrified).* Is that what this experiment has cost me, son? Has your freedom been paid for by a pair of eyes?

SEGISMUNDO. Is it the national pastime in Spain to speak in rhetorical questions?

BASILIO. My son, my prince...oh, the suffering you've already caused me! I came here expecting, hoping, that your good behavior would finally silence the arrogant stars...instead I walk in on a house of broken hearts and torment...a servant blinded...the blood on your indifferent hands still warm. With what love can I touch you, my son, knowing the pain those fingers have caused? I tremble knowing your hands are the instruments of torture, the articulators of blind fury. Don't touch me. I came here with my arms out, hoping to embrace you, to welcome you to the society of men, to give a father's love, to energize our nation with a swift reunion, and to finally thwart the jealous and untrue constellations...no, son...now I am afraid to look at you.

SEGISMUNDO. I can live without your arms, your embraces, and your fatherly love, Father—since I've lived without those things all my life. And I can live without the insipid rhetoric of love, Father! I used to ask Clotaldo: what does "father" mean? And he'd define it for me a hundred different ways. And I never got it, Father! You've kept me from your *side*... I've been no more than an *animal* to you...you've treated me like a malformation...an embarrassment...a godless spirit deprived of teaching, of laughter, of the violent colors of nature, of experience, of time and destiny. In the dirty war you've waged against me, in my two decades as a political prisoner, you have desired nothing less than my total mutilation...what do I care, Father, that you won't touch me now?

BASILIO. In the name of the Lord Jesus Christ, I ask only one thing: to never be reminded that I brought you into existence!

SEGISMUNDO. If you hadn't given me life, I wouldn't have been offended! But you did give me life—and you did take it away—and so you have offended me.

BASILIO. I freed you from the tower! I gave you freedom!

SEGISMUNDO. So you demand my gratitude? For what? What do I have to thank you for? You're an old and dying tyrant. What are you really giving me? As prince, this, all of this—the empire itself—is mine by *law*. I owe you nothing. In fact, you owe me for the stolen years of imprisonment and abuse.

BASILIO. Barbarian! Atrocity! Pillager! Living outrage!

CLARÍN. Eye-gouger!

BASILIO. The astrologers were right about you! The stars were understated! Be careful, Prince! You are the heir to this throne and the First Citizen of this state, but you must be humble and docile! Otherwise, be warned...you may be sleeping right now...and what you think is real may not be real...the power you enjoy may be nothing more substantial than the power of a dream... *(BASILIO and ASTOLFO exit.)*

SEGISMUNDO *(to CLARÍN).* The power of a dream! Is the old man crazy? Am I imagining all this? No! This isn't a dream! I touch things; I feel them. I am who I am! He'll regret what he said, you'll see! I disbelieve what I was and believe what I am: heir to the Crown, the wronged, much-deceived prince, back from political exile! If he kept me in darkness it was not because of my weakness but because I couldn't know who I was. But now I know exactly what I am, what I've turned into, courtesy of my dear dad: a crossbreed, a mixed-blood, a hybrid—half man, half animal.

(ROSAURA enters, dressed as a woman.)

ROSAURA. Estrella? Lady? Are you here?

SEGISMUNDO *(seeing her).* My God, who is that? *(SEGISMUNDO stares at ROSAURA, who doesn't see him and practices fencing moves in preparation for killing ASTOLFO.)*

CLARÍN. So...big guy...what do you like most about being rich and famous?

SEGISMUNDO. The women.

CLARÍN. No surprise there.

SEGISMUNDO. Nothing I've seen since my sudden awakening has filled me with more contradictory and untranslatable feelings. They look peaceful enough but they fill my inner heart with tempests and whirlwinds. They speak softly enough but their voices echo in my memory at such volume that my head would burst. I once read, in one of the many theological treatises I ate, that God gave His best gifts and focused His greatest creative energy on making Man. Man—with the strength of mountains, the depth of oceans, the brilliance of fire—is Earth itself in miniature. But I think it was Woman God really loved. Woman—with the mystery of clouds, the depth of outer space, and the strange fires of the Milky Way—is Heaven itself in miniature. Truly, the descent to Earth is to the ascent to Heaven as Man is to Woman...especially if she's the woman I'm looking at right now. *(ROSAURA sees SEGISMUNDO, gasps, and starts to leave.)* Stay, Lady, stay!

ROSAURA. I can't.

SEGISMUNDO. Don't bring in the sunlight of your presence only to flee and leave me in the cold shadow of night.

ROSAURA. Sunlight? Shadow? I don't know these words...

SEGISMUNDO *(recognizing her face)*. I don't believe what I see...

ROSAURA *(recognizing him)*. Neither do I, sire! Goodbye!

SEGISMUNDO. I've seen your face before, Lady.

ROSAURA. No, I don't think that's possible. *(To CLARÍN.) Is* it, you worthless peasant slave?

CLARÍN. Impossible! Sire, have you seen the beautiful girls who live in the West Wing of the palace?

SEGISMUNDO *(to ROSAURA)*. But I look at you as if I'm looking at my own redemption, my own *life*.

ROSAURA. I have a job to do, my prince.

SEGISMUNDO. Dear woman—the two most excellent words a man may use in a lifetime of speaking—dear woman: who are you? Without knowing anything about you, I know I love you. I know it because, somehow, we've met before—maybe in a dream, in one of my few dreams of happiness! Please don't leave without telling me your name.

ROSAURA *(trying to remember it)*. It's...

CLARÍN & ROSAURA. Agnes/Astrea.

ROSAURA. Astrea. And I belong to Princess Estrella. I am her servant, a low and minuscule working woman with a busy schedule... *(ROSAURA tries to leave. SEGISMUNDO stops her.)*

SEGISMUNDO. Don't tell me you're a servant. Tell me the truth instead.

ROSAURA *(trying to get past him)*. The truth?

SEGISMUNDO. I just don't understand how you—the obviously superior light, the greater beauty—should serve and honor that fading ragwoman Estrella. You, the real woman, should be empress here, not that counterfeit, pretending, transparent forgery of a woman. *(SEGISMUNDO touches her face. ROSAURA is frozen.)*

ROSAURA. Since I crave your respect, sire, please let silence be my eloquent reply. *(She pushes his hand away and starts to leave.)*

SEGISMUNDO. But you don't have to leave me! You understand what I'm trying to tell you!

ROSAURA. I understand it too well!

SEGISMUNDO. Then understand that all this coyness does nothing but provoke my anger, Lady! Any resistance from you makes me insane...

ROSAURA. Even if fury overcomes you, it can't destroy the respect and honor convention demands you have for me.

SEGISMUNDO. Convention! I blinded a man today, a nice man, a family man, probably had a house full of grandkids—kids he'll never see again—just to prove that I could do it! *(SEGISMUNDO grabs ROSAURA.)*

ROSAURA *(to CLARÍN)*. Bring someone, fool!

CLARÍN. Help!

SEGISMUNDO. I did it with these fingers! Fingers more than capable of stealing your precious chastity!

CLARÍN. Help!

ROSAURA *(struggling)*. Now I understand why the horoscopes said you'd desolate this kingdom and bring disgrace to your family and misery to your people! But what can the world expect from you? You're not really a man, except in name. Without a soul, without a heart, without reason, a language of curses, an appetite for slaughter—you're more *animal* than man...

CLARÍN. Help!

SEGISMUNDO. I spoke to you kindly! I used civilized phrases! I expect kindness and civility in return! Insult me and I have no choice but to answer you with the ultimate insult...

CLARÍN. Help! *(SEGISMUNDO starts to tear at ROSAURA's clothes.)*

ROSAURA. God help me!

(CLOTALDO enters.)

SEGISMUNDO. In this room, I am God and animal!

CLOTALDO. I must stop you, Prince, even if it means my death! *(CLOTALDO grabs ROSAURA from SEGISMUNDO. ROSAURA runs to CLARÍN, who holds her.)*

SEGISMUNDO *(to CLOTALDO)*. This is the second time you've provoked me, you pathetic, weak, old man!

CLOTALDO. There is no unlimited power, even for a prince! You must control this passion! You must civilize your heart! *(SEGISMUNDO draws his dagger. CLOTALDO kneels at SEGISMUNDO's feet and grabs SEGISMUNDO's dagger.)* Kneeling at your feet, I will save my life!

SEGISMUNDO. Take your hand away! *(SEGISMUNDO pulls his dagger away from CLOTALDO. The two men fight.)*

ROSAURA. Clotaldo's in danger! Please help!

(SEGISMUNDO knocks CLOTALDO to the floor. ASTOLFO enters and gets between SEGISMUNDO and CLOTALDO. ROSAURA and CLARÍN hide from ASTOLFO. They watch.)

ASTOLFO. But what is this, my prince? Is this how a king's sword is stained—with the cold blood of an old man?

SEGISMUNDO. His blood for my honor!

ASTOLFO. There's no honor in fighting a weaker man.

SEGISMUNDO. Then let me fight a stronger, if a stronger one exists! *(SEGISMUNDO draws his sword.)*

ASTOLFO. I may kill a member of the royal family in self-defense.

(ASTOLFO draws his sword. They duel. BASILIO and ESTRELLA enter.)

BASILIO. A duel? In my presence? What's happening here? *(ASTOLFO sheaths his weapon.)*

ASTOLFO. Nothing, sire. We may both sheath our swords without losing our honor now that we're in your presence.

SEGISMUNDO. *Much*, sir, even though you are present. I was about to slaughter that cringing old bastard over there...

BASILIO. With no respect for his old age?

CLOTALDO *(to BASILIO)*. It's only me, Your Majesty; this conflict is of no importance...

SEGISMUNDO *(to BASILIO)*. It's absurd to ask me to respect old age! It's even more absurd to ask me to respect you. Some day soon, as I walk to the throne room, I'll walk on a carpet made of your gray hair, old man. That's the only way to repay you for the way you raised me. *(SEGISMUNDO exits.)*

BASILIO. Before you take that walk, you'll return to your sleep, child. There you'll know that every good thing that's happened today happened in your imagination. *(BASILIO and CLOTALDO exit.)*

ASTOLFO. Isn't it interesting, dear Estrella, how the prophets of doom are never wrong? You'd be the world's greatest psychic if you always predicted the worst—just look at Segismundo. The stars were completely right about him. And isn't it interesting how the opposite never seems to happen—look at me, for instance. My stars have always been good. My horoscopes bristled with happy news: conquests, money, applause, good looks—and *love*— *most* of all, love. So why is it, Princess, that my stars were wrong while Segismundo's were right? Why is it that instead of the love promised to me by the zodiac all I've gotten lately is a cold shoulder and an empty bed?

ESTRELLA. Oh, give me a break. Ask the girl whose picture you wore around your neck, so close to your fickle heart, the day we met. Ask her to read your tea leaves, Astolfo. Ask her to do your Tarot cards! She's your confidante, your better self, your oracle, and your soulmate, not me. *(ROSAURA waits for ASTOLFO's answer.)*

ASTOLFO *(to ESTRELLA)*. I swear on my mother's eyes to exorcise that girl's devilish likeness from the sanctuary of my heart, dear princess. *(ROSAURA attempts to lunge at ASTOLFO, to tear him apart with her bare hands, but CLARÍN restrains her.)* The space left behind by the flight of that black angel will be filled with your light and likeness. You are brighter than the sun! An eclipser of the crab Nebula! I'll get the picture right now. I'll give it to you and you can destroy it. *(ASTOLFO exits.)*

ESTRELLA. Astrea!

ROSAURA. Your Ladyship! Employer! Visionary! You, who outfox the foxes of Spain!

ESTRELLA. I like you. You're the only woman in this murky cesspool of a palace I can trust with a really delicate matter.

ROSAURA. Your lowly slave doesn't deserve such honor.

ESTRELLA. Probably not, but I don't have much choice. All the girls around here hate me. Here's the thing. My cousin Astolfo is a man—I mean, he's *quite* a man—he's rich, royal, handsome, and, basically, the guy's got it where it counts. I mean, you're a not-too-bad-looking young woman...for a specimen of your class, I mean... I don't have to tell you about...blind sexual attraction... fantasies the likes of which you've never experienced before...cold showers in the middle of the night...having to replace the bed sheets every morning! He talks too much and his metaphors drive me a little crazy, but the Duke does something really wacky to my personal chemistry. Okay, but there's a problem. There's something standing in our way. The faithless hog—can you believe this?—keeps a badly colorized picture of an ex-girlfriend on a little gold chain.

CLARÍN *(sotto to ROSAURA)*. Who could that be?

ROSAURA *(sotto to CLARÍN)*. Me, *bruto*!

ESTRELLA. Being a princess, I can't stand even the smallest competition and I've told him to bring it to me. And he's so spastically in love with me, he agreed. But being a noblewoman it would be socially embarrassing to take the picture from him. That's where you come in. I want you to let Astolfo give you the picture, which you'll give to me, which I'll destroy thoroughly, okay? If you understand what love and all its humiliations are about, Astrea, you'll understand why I ask this of you. *(Exits.)*

ROSAURA. Oh God, I wish I didn't understand! Clarín, I need your advice. You have to tell me what to do!

CLARÍN. Advice is my forte, madam.

ROSAURA. I mean, who can figure this out? Who's got enough brainpower to keep up with the endless supply of nagging misfortunes in this damn place?

CLARÍN. Prudent reflection often yields an abundance of—

ROSAURA. I mean, does good old God just sit up there all day long, casually choosing the people He's going to pour extra misery on? Did I win some kind of perverse celestial lottery? I mean, what's a girl to do faced with these choices?

CLARÍN. Cooler heads may sort out the complexities...

ROSAURA. It's like capital "M" Misfortune is a strange variation of the mythological Phoenix. It burns itself out ruining your life until you're both consumed in its fire and out of *your* dead ashes it comes back to life, stronger, ready to do more damage, promote more carnage. An endless cycle of regurgitated despair!

CLARÍN. I'm drawing a complete blank.

ROSAURA. Come on, Clarín! If I tell everyone who I really am, then Clotaldo, who saved my life, and holds his honor around me like a shield, and has asked me to sit passively by and say nothing and just wait, may be offended. And we know how bad offense is around here. But... if I don't tell Astolfo who I really am, and he sees me, how am I supposed to fool him? I'll deny to his face that I'm Rosaura, but he'll see the truth in my eyes—my soul will give me away through my eyes—dammit—if I could just poke them out! That's it, Clarín, honor depends on blindness! If I could just find a pin to plunge into my eyes, I could save myself... *(ROSAURA starts to search her clothes for a long pin.)*

CLARÍN. Madam!

ROSAURA *(looking at him).* You're right, what's the point? Whatever I do is only going to make things worse. It's my fate, wise Clarín, thank you for making that clear to me. It's my atrocious horoscope! I should just surrender to it. Let it win. Let it take me. Let this tortured soap opera reach its bloody climax and be done with it!

(ASTOLFO enters, holding ROSAURA's picture. ROSAURA pushes CLARÍN offstage. CLARÍN hides and watches.)

ASTOLFO *(amazed, to ROSAURA)*. I don't believe this.

ROSAURA. What's the matter? Something wrong with you?

ASTOLFO. That voice. That legendary face. Through the windows of those eyes, I see the soul of my dear love Rosaura.

ROSAURA. Me? Rosaura? Your eyes play tricks on you, sir. My name is Astrea.

ASTOLFO. Drop it, Rosaura, it's pointless. The soul doesn't lie. Not to one as deeply in love as I am. *(ASTOLFO tries to kiss ROSAURA. She pushes him away.)*

ROSAURA. Sir, Estrella—a woman Aphrodite herself would be proud to imitate—ordered me to ask you to give me that picture you hold in your hand.

ASTOLFO. Try that again. This time tell your eyes to play along with you. Tell your voice to convince itself before it tries to convince me. Come on, Rosaura, once more from the top! "Sir, Estrella—a woman Aphrodite herself..."

ROSAURA *(blushing with anger)*. ...would be proud to imitate—ordered me...

ASTOLFO. Very well. If you want to play games, we'll play games. "Ass-trea," was it? Ass-trea, as Duke of Warsaw, I command you to trot your tight little *Ass*-trea over to the princess, immediately, and tell her I honor her so much, I refuse to send her a mere *copy* of the beautiful Rosaura. Instead I'm going to send her the *original*: you.

ROSAURA. Sir. Originals are worth more than copies, true. But when an honorable person goes off having promised to perform a deed and then returns without having accomplished that deed—even if she returns with

something of greater worth—then that person is a liar
and a promise-breaker. And liars and promise-breakers
have a special place reserved for them in the *Inferno* of
my heart. I promised to get that picture from you and I
will get that picture from you right now!

ASTOLFO. No.

ROSAURA. Damn you! I spit in your father's sperm! *(She
tries to grab the picture as she and ASTOLFO tussle.)*

ASTOLFO. 'Tis a fiery little bitch!

ROSAURA. I'll kill us both before another woman—espe-
cially that simpleton—touches this picture of me!

ASTOLFO. I'm enjoying this tussle, Rosaura!

*(ASTOLFO has ROSAURA on her back. He lies on top
of her. ESTRELLA enters.)*

ESTRELLA. Astolfo, Astrea—what's all this tussling?

ASTOLFO. Estrella's here!

ROSAURA. Aren't you brilliant? *(To ESTRELLA.)* Lady,
my lady, my lady...I can explain this, just give me a
moment to order my thoughts.

ASTOLFO *(panicking)*. What are you going to say?

ROSAURA *(to ESTRELLA)*. You ordered me to wait here
for Astolfo and ask him for that picture. I was alone.
And, being alone, you know, the mind wanders, day-
dreams assert themselves, and since we were talking of
pictures, I remembered I had one of myself, here, hidden
in my sleeve. Crazy with boredom I took it out to look
at it and I dropped it.

ASTOLFO. She dropped it.

ROSAURA. Shut up. *(To ESTRELLA.)* Astolfo the Brilliant, as he's referred to by the epic poets of Warsaw,

came along with the picture of that other girl, ready to surrender it to you via me, and he saw my picture on the floor. And he's so adamantly opposed to giving you the picture of his sexy ex-lover that he actually intends to give you *my* picture instead! Which I can't let him do. When he wouldn't give me my picture, we tussled briefly for it.

ASTOLFO. I didn't enjoy that part at all.

ROSAURA. The picture *Ass*-tolfo is holding in his hand is mine. Look at it... whose face do you see?

ESTRELLA *(to ASTOLFO)*. Give me the picture.

ASTOLFO. Do I have to? *(ESTRELLA grabs the picture from ASTOLFO and looks at it.)*

ESTRELLA. She's a true beauty with a dangerous and fiery soul—and your twin, Astrea. Take it and get out of here. *(ESTRELLA gives ROSAURA her picture.)*

ROSAURA. Now ask him for the other one, miss. *(Exits.)*

ESTRELLA. Give me the picture I requested. Though I'll never look at it or refer to it again, I don't want it in your hands. Since I disgraced myself by asking for it, it has to be destroyed.

ASTOLFO. I live to serve you, you know that, oh gorgeous one, but I can't, I can't, don't make me...

ESTRELLA. You're a lying heathen and a shitty lover! I don't want you to give it to me! If I had it, it would only remind me how I begged you for it! *(ESTRELLA exits.)*

ASTOLFO *(to ESTRELLA)*. Does that mean the engagement's off? *(To himself.)* Rosaura, Rosaura—*Rosaura!* *(Blackout.)*

SCENE TWO

SETTING: *The tower.*

AT RISE: *SEGISMUNDO, wearing animal skins, asleep, is being chained to the walls by the masked 1st, 2nd, and 3rd GUARDS. CLOTALDO and CLARÍN watch. CLOTALDO is holding his mask.*

CLOTALDO *(to SEGISMUNDO)*. Here you'll stay. Your tragedy ends where it began.

CLARÍN *(to SEGISMUNDO)*. As soon as you awaken, young prince, you'll understand what you've lost. Good luck has painfully mutated into its opposite. Your glory was pretended, your life was a fool's shadow, and your new destiny is death.

CLOTALDO *(to the GUARDS, indicating CLARÍN)*. Lock him up. *(The GUARDS grab CLARÍN.)*

CLARÍN. Me? What did I do?

CLOTALDO. State secrets, national security—you understand—can't be trusted to someone with a mouth like yours.

CLARÍN. Correct me if I'm wrong, but did I threaten to kill my father? Did I squeeze out the eyes of a poor servant? Jesus, am I awake or am I dreaming?

CLOTALDO. Your big mouth has ruined you—are you so surprised?

(The GUARDS take CLARÍN away. BASILIO enters, disguised.)

BASILIO. Trusted friend.

CLOTALDO. Sire? Is that you?

BASILIO. Stupid curiosity of mine. I came to see what's become of my son.

CLOTALDO. Closer to the animals than to God.

BASILIO. Demolished prince, forgive me. What can I do? The stars predicted your misconduct. I have no choice if I'm to save my country.

SEGISMUNDO *(dreaming)*. Eagles! Violent, necessary birds! I'm with you now! I'm your prince. Prince of the Skies! Prince of Freedom! *(SEGISMUNDO starts to wake up. Wiping tears from his eyes, BASILIO starts to exit.)*

BASILIO *(to CLOTALDO)*. I can't let the child see me. I'll hide. *(He hides. CLOTALDO puts on his mask. SEGISMUNDO wakes up.)*

SEGISMUNDO. What am I doing here? Where's the palace? Where are my clothes? Where are the servants? Am I back in the tower? God of Love, what have I been dreaming?

CLOTALDO. Ah! You've finally awakened.

SEGISMUNDO. Have I?

CLOTALDO. I was starting to think you were going to sleep all day. You fell asleep the moment you saw that eagle flying by.

SEGISMUNDO. But I think I must still be sleeping and dreaming! If I *have* been dreaming—what I dreamed seemed so true—it makes me doubt what I see right now. This tower, these chains, *this* must be the dream!

CLOTALDO. I don't understand you...

SEGISMUNDO. If I was dreaming...I don't know if I can tell you about it. No, it *wasn't* a dream. I *saw* those things. I woke up and I saw a bed of bright colors, like flowers, as if I were waking up in a garden of pleasures. Dozens of servants and pretty ladies dressed me in jewels and called me Prince. You, Clotaldo, you said I was the heir to the Spanish throne!

CLOTALDO. What did I get for telling you the good news?

SEGISMUNDO. I tried to kill you—twice!

CLOTALDO *(laughs)*. Twice!

SEGISMUNDO. I learned I had always been Prince. So I sought revenge on everyone responsible for my years in exile. *(Beat.)* Except for one. A woman I loved. Loving her must have really happened to me. Hers is the one memory I still have on my skin... not the eyes of the poor man I crippled. Why, Clotaldo? Why did I dream those things? *(BASILIO leaves his hiding place and exits, wiping his eyes.)*

CLOTALDO. We were talking about eagles as you fell asleep. So you dreamed of power. Let me tell you something. Even in dreams you should honor those who gave you life and raised you. Even in dreams you must do what's right.

SEGISMUNDO. That's true. And since we're dreaming now, let me bury my animal side, as well as my anger and ambition. In this enchanted world, this world of mirages, to simply live is to dream. And since life is a dream, I know we don't truly wake up until we die. The king dreams he's the king and he rules and governs without knowing that all the praises he receives on loan are written in the wind and are soon turned to ashes and death. Who'd *want* to be king knowing that when he dies he's going to wake up and be nothing? Rich men dream of money—but money brings more grief than pleasure. The poor man dreams of his endlessly shrinking stomach. The pretender, the anarchist, the child, the ancient scholar, the pious, the lonely—all of them are dreamers—and none of them understands the dream! I dream I'm sitting in this muck, a convict—but I dreamed earlier I was happy, alive, powerful. Which was real? What is life? A frenzy. What is living? An illusion, a shadow, a fiction. The greatest good is nothing but a weightless idea. To live is to sleep, to live is to dream, all who live are dreamers, all dreamers are the dreams of God, and what is God Himself, but the greatest dream of all? *(Blackout.)*

END OF ACT TWO

ACT THREE

SCENE ONE

SETTING: *The tower. The sun and moon are visible in the sky.*

AT RISE: *CLARÍN is chained to the wall.*

CLARÍN. *Ay misero de mi! Y ay infelice!*
VOICES *(off)*. Shut up! Quit your whining! Shut your hole! I'll give you something to cry about!
CLARÍN. I can't shut up! My name means "trumpet"— and I've got to trumpet my woes all over Creation!
VOICE *(off)*. At least they haven't started torturing you! Just wait 'till you see what they do to your balls!
CLARÍN. HELP MEEEEEE! I'm trapped in a haunted tower! Buried alive because I know too much! Starving. Lonely, except for the rats and roaches. All my prospects, my old age, my retirement, up in smoke. Poor, pathetic, incarcerated me! Sapped, sacked, stolen, swollen me! And I'm having some really bad dreams here. Nightmares huddle around my soft, old brain. Oh, the things I've seen in my sleep. Crucified virgins! Tortured martyrs! All night my dreamself looks upon blood and gore and all night I faint and gag. Now that I'm awake, I faint from HUNGER, from SILENCE. I've become the patron saint of voicelessness. The shadow God of oblivion and secrets. *(The sound of drums. Many VOICES offstage.)*

1st SOLDIER *(off)*. This is the cell where they're keeping him! Smash this door!

CLARÍN. Oh good, more miseries!

(Sound of doors being burst open. 1st, 2nd, 3rd SOLDIERS enter and see CLARÍN.)

1st SOLDIER. There he is!

CLARÍN. No he isn't! Please! Don't torture me! I know you Spanish excel at it! But I hate the smell of my flesh burning! And please don't hurt my testicles! *(The SOLDIERS bow to CLARÍN.)*

1st SOLDIER. Your mighty Lordship!

CLARÍN. Oh, great, they're drunk too!

1st SOLDIER. Prince of Spain! We will fight and die under the banner of a native-born Prince of Spain...but never under the colors of a foreigner! Men, kiss his feet. *(The SOLDIERS kiss CLARÍN's feet.)*

CLARÍN. Stop it, that's really disgusting.

SOLDIERS. Long live our glorious prince!

CLARÍN. So let me get this straight. It's actually a tradition in Spain to take wretched prisoners out of jail and make them Head of State?

1st SOLDIER. We've told your father the king that we'll recognize only you as our sovereign leader—not that foreign usurper Astolfo, Duke of Warsaw.

CLARÍN. My father's the king?

1st SOLDIER *(to other SOLDIERS)*. He's delirious from the constant torture and bad food...and being in this tower has aged him badly. Those criminals in Basilio's gang will pay for this, Your Lordship. Long live Prince Segismundo!

SOLDIERS. Long live Prince Segismundo! *(The SOLDIERS break CLARÍN's chains and set him free.)*

CLARÍN. I get it now. Every guy you do this to is renamed Segismundo. Okay! I love that name!

(SEGISMUNDO enters, his arms and legs chained.)

SEGISMUNDO. Who calls my name? Who calls Segismundo?

CLARÍN. Oh shit.

1st SOLDIER. Wait a minute. Will the real Segismundo please make yourself known to us.

SEGISMUNDO. I am Segismundo.

CLARÍN. *Ay Dios*, I'm screwed.

1st SOLDIER *(to CLARÍN)*. How dare you impersonate the Prince of Spain!

CLARÍN. Me? You're the one who re-baptized me Segismundo!

1st SOLDIER *(to SEGISMUNDO)*. Fair prince. Your father lied to you. You were not dreaming when you were in the palace. They drugged you and dragged you out of prison and put you on the throne denied to you by the vicious ignorance of the stars. When they didn't like what happened they drugged you again and re-imprisoned you. Now the incogitant king and his senile staff wish to give our fair Castile to foreigners! To Polacks! But the people, hearing that a true native-born prince exists, have risen up against your father. We have come in vast numbers, a true guerrilla army of bandits and peasants, to give you freedom and fight at your side.

VOICES *(off)*. Long live Prince Segismundo!

SEGISMUNDO. *¿Otra vez? ¿Que es esto, cielo?* God, am I dreaming again? Must I suffer this recurring dream, over and over, until I die? Am I to be overjoyed by the promise of great power and fame—only to lose it all again? No, you can't make me hope again, only to take it away. In a prison like this, in a life like this, hope is too risky. I know that life is a dream. I know that you floating, insubstantial men are the shades and handpuppets of an evil Dreamer—a God determined to make me crazy! Yes, I know you well! And I know myself: I'm a sleeping man sick of pretended sovereignty and make-believe fame and simulations and masks! I'm wise now and you can't deceive me anymore!

1st SOLDIER. If you think we're illusory, look out that window, gaze at the carpeted mountains, and see the population of a great dominion assembled to honor you. Great events in history, my lord, are often foretold in dreams. The premonitions, *deja vu*, and shadows of the mind are often truer than reality. If you've already dreamed all this, then your vision was a mere prologue to the grandest turning point in our history. As I live and breathe, good prince, this moment lives, seize it now before it passes.

SEGISMUNDO. You speak well...that's a dangerous quality in a man of action. Perhaps you're right. Perhaps my dream was a preindication—an inspiration—to my waking self. And if not—if our short life is but a dream—so be it. Let's dream then. And let's be aware that our pleasure could all disappear at a moment's notice. Let's remember that all is temporary. All life is borrowed and must be returned. Knowing this, let's risk it all, my loyal soldiers, and not be afraid. Let's dream of conquest and justice! Let's dream of armies and liberation! Let's dream of honor and sweet revenge! Let's show Basilio just how right his astrologers were!

SOLDIERS. *¡Viva* Segismundo, *viva!*

SEGISMUNDO. And death to foreigners!

SOLDIERS. Death to foreigners!

(The SOLDIERS break SEGISMUNDO's chains and set him free. CLOTALDO enters, masked.)

CLOTALDO. What is this? What's happening here?

CLARÍN *(to CLOTALDO)*. You better cover those eyes, boss!

CLOTALDO *(taking off his mask)*. Now that you're free again, and powerful, surrounded by loyal soldiers...I know you have to kill me for what I've done to you. All I ask is you do it quickly and tell the world I did not beg for mercy. *(CLOTALDO kneels.)*

SEGISMUNDO. *Levanta, levanta, padre...* *(SEGISMUNDO helps CLOTALDO to his feet.)* ...my true father. You raised me, taught me, strengthened me in a world that would have wasted me otherwise—let me embrace you in gratitude. *(SEGISMUNDO embraces CLOTALDO.)*

CLOTALDO. What is this?

SEGISMUNDO. A dream, of course. But this is a dream I will control. You said yourself, even in dreams we must do what's right. So I will dream humility and generosity toward those I owe my life to and destruction and hopelessness toward everyone else...my father most of all.

CLOTALDO. In the spirit of doing what's right—if that's your credo—you have to understand what I must do. I can't go against your father. I can't march in your army. Basilio is my king and my friend and like everyone in the kingdom—including you men—I owe him absolute and unconditional loyalty. If that makes me a threat, Segismundo, then do what you have to do to punish me.

SEGISMUNDO. You're an old idiot, Clotaldo, and a fool! *(SEGISMUNDO takes a SOLDIER's sword and raises it as if to strike CLOTALDO.)* The nerves and demons in my body beg me to silence you...but I won't. No one deserves to die for being loyal. And just knowing this is a dream checks my passion and inhibits me. I know when I wake up again, I'll see you here, bringing me food and books...

CLOTALDO. My prince...

SEGISMUNDO. Go. Obey your loyalty. Do what common sense tells you. Don't stand here arguing with us—every man has his own definition of honor.

CLOTALDO. I must fight for the Spain of King Basilio.

SEGISMUNDO. Then I'll see you on the battlefield, my friend.

CLOTALDO. On the battlefield. *(CLOTALDO and SEGISMUNDO embrace, kiss. CLOTALDO exits.)*

SEGISMUNDO *(kneeling in prayer)*. Don't wake me up, dear God, don't do it. If I'm awake, don't let me fall asleep. Whether we're shadows or not, it's important to do what's right and what's honorable. Let's go! *(Blackout.)*

SCENE TWO

SETTING: *The palace. The sun and moon are closer together.*

AT RISE: *BASILIO and ASTOLFO are suiting up for battle.*

BASILIO. Who can stop the furious charge of a horse gone wild? That's what my people have become! Inflamed adolescents! Gangsters and sycophants! They disappoint me greatly! Half the country is screaming, "Long live Astolfo!" The other half is crying, "Long live Segismundo!" Rioting and destruction is all they know to give me, when they should be giving me loyalty, obedience, and taxes! It's anarchy! We might as well be living in France!

ASTOLFO. Today was to be my coronation day, a day I've waited for all my life. I'm not going to let a mob of unclean paupers ruin it! They want tough? They want a little demonstration of ruthlessness? They want to see if I have the right stuff to be king? Someone get my horse ready!

BASILIO *(fighting tears).* It's all my fault. This had all been predicted and I tried to sneak around the stars and they've come back to punish me. The more I tried to avoid it, the worse it became. I've destroyed my own kingdom, Astolfo.

(BASILIO cries. ASTOLFO exits. ESTRELLA enters.)

ESTRELLA. Cry. Fine. Good way to stop the bloodletting, Uncle! *Stop that!* I've got such a headache! Today was supposed to be my wedding day. I was supposed to be crowned Queen today. Instead I'm watching effigies of myself burning all over Madrid! Christ, do something! I'm watching eyes being torn out of faces. I'm seeing common street corners turning into instant graves. I'm seeing the proliferation of orphans and ghosts. Every flower in the kingdom covers someone's tomb. Every citizen is an accomplice to murder. Those not killed in the fire of this civil war are choked by the smoke of unbearable sorrow...

BASILIO *(controlling himself)*. Yes. And it must be brought to a sudden ending.

ESTRELLA. And another eclipse threatens to swallow the world.

BASILIO *(calling out)*. My horse! I will slaughter my upstart son myself if that's what it takes to save the kingdom!

ESTRELLA. Please let me fight with you! I was born for combat!

BASILIO. Come, Princess! Every soldier is welcome!

(BASILIO and ESTRELLA exit. ROSAURA enters, pursued by CLOTALDO.)

ROSAURA. Everything is war! War is everything!

CLOTALDO. What are you going to do?

ROSAURA. This war gives me the chance to do what I've waited much too long to do: to kill Astolfo, Duke of Warsaw.

CLOTALDO. Kill the man destined to be the next king of Spain?

ROSAURA. Until then he's just the bastard who wronged me.

CLOTALDO. My girl, you're lost! You're determined to die!

ROSAURA. So be it. My good name inspires me to this, Clotaldo. My self-respect implores me. My anger justifies me. There's no other way, good sir, there's no other way! *(ROSAURA exits. Blackout.)*

SCENE THREE

SETTING: *An open field. Upstage, a pile of rocks. The sun and moon are approaching total eclipse.*

AT RISE: *SEGISMUNDO is wearing animal skins. SOLDIERS and CLARÍN are at his side.*

SEGISMUNDO. *¡Si este dia me viera Roma!* Rome would see a resurrected barbarian lifting his sword to command the world's greatest army! Flattening the fortresses of Heaven would be too easy! But no, good soldiers. I should be careful. Such arrogant language could hurt me. If I awaken...and all of this has been an illusion, then I'll be bitter and lost...

CLARÍN. Look! A beautiful woman on a dappled horse! Or is that a dappled woman on a beautiful horse? Or a dappled horse on a beautiful woman? Or a...?

SEGISMUNDO. She's brilliant, lucent...

CLARÍN. Hold on, it's Rosaura.

SEGISMUNDO. God's brought her back to me.

(ROSAURA enters, dressed in the traditional skirts of a peasant woman, but armed to the teeth.)

ROSAURA. Generous Prince! You've been reincarnated from shadows and awakened to a new life, like a new sun rising over a glorious New World. Please let an unfortunate woman speak with you. Please let my status and my sex inspire your compassion and your chivalry. *(Beat.)* Three times you've seen me in three incarnations. The first time, I was dressed as a man. I met you in the tower and you were an animal with a man's heart and your troubles made mine look small and I pitied you. The second time, you saw me as a woman, a low servant, and you were the most resplendent and horrifying of kings. Indeed, in that grim nightmare afternoon you were a man with an animal's heart. This is the third meeting, and today I am both man and woman, dressed for war as a man, but containing a woman's broken heart. Today I am myself. *(Beat.)* Sir, my father left Poland, and my beautiful mother Violante, years ago— leaving behind only his sparkling sword and her shattered hope. He dishonored her by leaving her, despite his many promises, unwed, and pregnant with me. I was the result of a young man's charming words and a young woman's willingness to believe, and if I haven't inherited my mother's beauty, I have inherited her luck: I too have been dishonored by a man. It was the Duke Astolfo of Warsaw. Just saying that faithless name—look at me!—is enough to inspire tears of hatred. Indeed, for a long time, after he loved me and left me to colonize his cousin, I went insane. I'd swear I'd hear my thoughts spoken aloud by village savants who had kidnapped my mind. I ate dirt. I cut my arms. I lay in bed counting spiders. I developed a hatred of even numbers. If I counted an even number of spiders, I'd eat one. I tried to kill myself several times. I lost the power to speak! It was my mother who brought me back from the dead: my mother told me her own pitiful story and that's when I decided to live—and to avenge her honor as well as mine—that's when I decided this cycle of rape and abandonment would end with me. Shielded with my mother's blessings and armed with my father's sword, I came to Spain and now I've come to you. *(Beat.)* You have a chance to avenge the wrongs done to you. You are justified in the eyes of God and man. I ask you to let me stand at your side, to fight at your side, and let me find my revenge, let the field of combat be the site of my life's recovery. Sir, you know it's vital to both of us that Astolfo and Estrella not marry. I've come here to serve you with my woman's spirit and my manly sword, but if you try to seduce me as a woman, I'll cut your throat as a man. If that's understood, generous Segismundo, let's proceed into battle and win this war of love.

SEGISMUNDO. How is it possible for you to know so much about my dream? All those things you mentioned were the shadows of my sleeping life—impossible for you to know—unless, it had never been a dream...

ROSAURA. It was all true. I was there.

CLARÍN. So was I.

SEGISMUNDO *(to ROSAURA)*. I'll help you restore your honor, by the God of Love, I will! Sound the alarms! *(Sound of trumpets. SEGISMUNDO addresses his SOLDIERS:)* Ultimately we can't know what's real and what isn't. How do we know that every past moment of happiness and glory wasn't dreamed? How do we know that all happiness will not end in disenchantment? How do we know that death isn't the final awakening? And when we finally awaken and look into the face of the Dreamer who made us all, what will we see there? All questions are unanswerable. All truths are unknowable. All is confusion and chaos! In this anarchy of the mind, let's try to find some hope and happiness and love. Let's do it before love turns to sorrow. Let's do it in the brief time we have on Earth. Above all, let's try to win some glory and let's hope it lasts a few good moments, if not forever!

ROSAURA. Segismundo! I'll fight with you!

SEGISMUNDO. Dear woman, I'll avenge your honor before I seize the crown. *(Trumpets. SEGISMUNDO and SOLDIERS exit. Before she can exit, ROSAURA is stopped by CLARÍN.)*

CLARÍN. Before you go, madam, I have to tell you what I've learned. I know a secret! I know who you are! I know Clotaldo is— *(Battle sounds: trumpets, cannons, shots, screams.)*

ROSAURA. Segismundo's being attacked! He's surrounded! I can't be afraid, Clarín! I must be at his side! *(Exits.)*

VOICES *(off)*. Long live Astolfo!

VOICES *(off)*. Long live Segismundo!

CLARÍN. Long live Astolfo and Segismundo! Long live everybody! Stop the fighting, you assholes! Ugh, look at yourselves. All that waste. Shame on all of you! *(A bullet whizzes over CLARÍN's head and he hits the ground.)* I better shut up and get my ass to some safe hiding place—away from all this unrestricted hooliganism and machismo! Some place where Death will never find me!

(CLARÍN crawls to the upstage rocks and hides behind them. SOLDIERS from both armies enter and fight. SOLDIERS exit. BASILIO, CLOTALDO, ASTOLFO, and ESTRELLA enter—all are bloody.)

BASILIO. Has there ever been an unhappier king? A more disrespected father?

CLOTALDO. Your army's in full retreat...

ASTOLFO. The traitors are winning!

ESTRELLA. Loyalists and patriots are the ones who win wars. *We're* the traitors now, Astolfo...

BASILIO. We must escape to the New World before Segismundo finds me. *(Shots are fired. CLARÍN falls from behind the rocks. He staggers downstage, mortally wounded.)*

CLARÍN. Fucking great! Oh this is bloody brilliant!

ASTOLFO. Who is this clown?

CLARÍN. Oh, just some joker who thought he could run away from Death and ran smack into it. Oh, this hurts. This is mortal! I have some advice. Next time you want to avoid dying in war, run smack into the middle of the battlefield. Don't go hiding behind tons of protective granite. 'Cause, I'll tell you, if God really *wants* your ass, He's going to get your ass... *(CLARÍN dies.)*

ESTRELLA. "If God really wants your ass, He's going to get your ass."

CLOTALDO. What strange eloquence!

BASILIO. The clown's right. The more you run from Fate, the quicker it finds you. It's foolish to run from the decrees of God and the stars.

CLOTALDO. True, but a wise man must try. Stars may prove false. And God's will is often ambiguous and subject to interpretation. Let's run.

ASTOLFO. Clotaldo's right. We should run, my lord. He'll protect us as we go.

BASILIO. No. If God's verdict is "Death," then Death is what I'll face, here, in the heart of my country, in the midst of the terror I created.

(BASILIO, CLOTALDO, and ESTRELLA exit. ROSAURA enters. ROSAURA attacks ASTOLFO.)

ROSAURA. Rapist!

(ROSAURA and ASTOLFO fight. ROSAURA stabs ASTOLFO with the ornate sword. He falls, wounded. She stands over him, ready to strike again. ESTRELLA runs to ASTOLFO and covers his body, looking up at ROSAURA, angry eyes pleading for mercy. The sun and moon are in total eclipse. ROSAURA throws the ornate sword away. She sees CLARÍN, lets out a cry, and prays over his body. BASILIO and CLOTALDO enter, chased by Segismundo's SOLDIERS. They surround BASILIO. BASILIO kneels as SEGISMUNDO enters.)

BASILIO. If you're looking for me, here, find me in the dirt, my son. Take my gray hairs and wipe your feet on them. Step on my back on your way to the throne. Take my disgraced crown, my broken reputation, and my sullied honor and destroy them all. Make a slave of your senile parent and you'll finally fulfill the promise of the stars.

SEGISMUNDO. Listen to me, all of you. Whatever God writes in the book of destiny is final. It can't be rewritten. It can only be misinterpreted. My father tried to save himself from the words of destiny and, in so doing, turned me into an animal—though it was possible, had I had a normal childhood and had I been able to cherish my natural gifts and sharpen my intelligence, I would have grown up to be a fair and tolerant monarch. We'll never know. By trying to keep me from being wild, he made me wild! If someone told you this sword would kill you, would you deliberately put it to your throat? Injustice and revenge will not help you overcome your fate—only reason, tolerance, and tranquility of spirit will. Let all of you who are watching this conquest remember it as the illustration of the astrologers' predictions: a kingdom left bleeding, a royal family compromised, and a good king reduced to slavery. All of it has come to pass. How am I, who am younger, and spiritually weaker than this man, able to overcome the fate he could not? *(Beat.)* King Basilio, stand. Let me take your hand, dear father. Now that you're enlightened and know your errors—here I am—I kneel before you and surrender myself and my treasonous armies to your authority—take your revenge on us as you see fit. *(BASILIO stands. SEGISMUNDO kneels at BASILIO's feet.)*

BASILIO. You're my son. Such incredible mercy and wisdom—you're my proper son—again! You've conquered this nation in legitimate battle—and pardoned me in a noble act of compassion—you've truly earned the right to be called King of Spain.

ALL. Long live King Segismundo!

SEGISMUNDO *(to BASILIO)*. The legitimate battle I've fought today hasn't been on the naked earth or under the judgmental sky, but in my tumultuous spirit, where a war between a bestial nature and a human one has been waging since birth. I've won a great victory over myself today. *(To the others.)* Clotaldo will be fully pardoned for all the years of my incarceration. Astolfo and Estrella will be restored to their proper places in the royal family. They will wed immediately.

ESTRELLA & ASTOLFO. Thank you, my lord.

SEGISMUNDO. And Clarín will be buried with full military honors.

1st SOLDIER. And the tower?

SEGISMUNDO. Level it. Erase it. Consign it to memory and never build another one. *(SOLDIERS carry away CLARÍN. ESTRELLA, ASTOLFO, BASILIO, and CLOTALDO exit. ROSAURA approaches SEGISMUNDO.)*

ROSAURA. My king? What about me?

SEGISMUNDO. I have two regrets: I'm sorry I ever raised a hand against you in lustful anger; I'm sorry I tried to crush your spirit. If you can, please forgive me.

ROSAURA. You were insane then. Seeing how much you've changed, how wise and gentle you are, I can forgive you.

SEGISMUNDO. Dear woman—nearly sister and twin...

ROSAURA. Don't call me sister. A sister can't do this. *(ROSAURA kisses SEGISMUNDO.)*

SEGISMUNDO. My second regret, dear Rosaura, is this: now that I know I'm the king's son, I don't think I'm able to love you and wed you as I wish, because you're not of noble birth...

(CLOTALDO enters.)

CLOTALDO. Rosaura is a noblewoman, Your Majesty, as highly born as any in Europe. Rosaura, I'm the man who dishonored Violante, your mother—may she forgive me someday. I'm your father.

ROSAURA. I think I've always known it, sir. *(ROSAURA embraces CLOTALDO. He exits. She turns to SEGISMUNDO, who walks away from her.)* What's wrong?

SEGISMUNDO. What if...? Rosaura, I'm afraid...what if I wake up too soon...and all this is once again a shadow's shadow and I'm found alone, screaming in a prison cell...

ROSAURA. Don't say it. Don't question it. Just let it happen to you. If it's a dream, good. Perhaps I'll wake up myself. Perhaps all this is my dream, with you in it. Either way we can let our dreams teach us about the brevity of life and the fleeting nature of happiness. If life *isn't* a dream—and I don't think it is—even better. We make it what we want. We stay and build on the past. Or we forego royalty and go to the New World to start over. If *la vida no es sueño*...that means this is it, my prince, my love. This is the one. This is the only life there is. *(SEGISMUNDO and ROSAURA kiss. The eclipse ends. Bright sunlight. Blackout.)*

END OF PLAY

DIRECTOR'S NOTES

DIRECTOR'S NOTES

DIRECTOR'S NOTES

DIRECTOR'S NOTES

DIRECTOR'S NOTES